Please

Kelly Doudna

Published by SandCastle™, an imprint of ABDO Publishing Company, 4940 Viking Drive, Edina, Minnesota 55435.

Printed in the United States.

Cover and interior photo credits: Eyewire Images, Digital Stock, PhotoDisc, Stock Market

Library of Congress Cataloging-in-Publication Data

Doudna, Kelly, 1963-
    Please / Kelly Doudna.
       p. cm. -- (Good manners)
    Includes index.
    ISBN 1-57765-570-2
       1. Courtesy--Juvenile literature. 2. Children--Conduct of life. 3. Etiquette. [1.
Etiquette.] I. Title.

    BJ1533.C9 .D687 2001
    395.1'22--dc21

                                                                    2001022001

The SandCastle concept, content, and reading method have been reviewed and approved by a national advisory board including literacy specialists, librarians, elementary school teachers, early childhood education professionals, and parents.

Let Us Know

After reading the book, SandCastle would like you to tell us your stories about reading. What is your favorite page? Was there something hard that you needed help with? Share the ups and downs of learning to read. We want to hear from you! To get posted on the ABDO Publishing Company Web site, send us email at:

sandcastle@abdopub.com

About SandCastle™

Nonfiction books for the beginning reader

- Basic concepts of phonics are incorporated with integrated language methods of reading instruction. Most words are short, and phrases, letter sounds, and word sounds are repeated.

- Readability is determined by the number of words in each sentence, the number of characters in each word, and word lists based on curriculum frameworks.

- Full-color photography reinforces word meanings and concepts.

- "Words I Can Read" list at the end of each book teaches basic elements of grammar, helps the reader recognize the words in the text, and builds vocabulary.

- Reading levels are indicated by the number of flags on the castle.

Look for more SandCastle books in these three reading levels:

Level 1 (one flag)	**Level 2** (two flags)	**Level 3** (three flags)

Grades Pre-K to K 5 or fewer words per page	**Grades K to 1** 5 to 10 words per page	**Grades 1 to 2** 10 to 15 words per page

We say the word "please" when we ask for something.

Saying "**please**" when we ask for something shows that we have good manners.

Ping watches while her dad cooks.

She says, "I would like a hot dog please."

Hal is helping chop
vegetables.

His dad says, "The knife is
sharp. **Please** be careful."

Mark is making a model.

He asks, "Would you please pass the glue?"

Faith follows her sister.

She calls out, "**Please** wait for me!"

Maria wants to make
a jack-o-lantern.

She asks, "May we buy
a pumpkin **please**?"

Dan talks to his dad.

His mom asks, "May I **please** speak with him?"

Lola would like to leave the table.

How should she ask?

Words I Can Read

Nouns

A noun is a person, place, or thing

dad (DAD) pp. 9, 11, 19

glue (GLOO) p. 13

hot dog
  (HOT DAWG) p. 9

jack-o-lantern
  (JAK-uh-lan-turn) p. 17

knife (NIFE) p. 11

model (MOD-uhl) p. 13

mom (MOM) p. 19

pumpkin
  (PUHMP-kin) p. 17

sister (SISS-tur) p. 15

table (TAY-buhl) p. 21

word (WURD) p. 5

Proper Nouns

A proper noun is the name
of a person, place, or thing

Dan (DAN) p. 19

Faith (FAYTH) p. 15

Hal (HAL) p. 11

Lola (LOH-luh) p. 21

Maria
  (muh-REE-uh) p. 17

Mark (MARK) p. 13

Ping (PING) p. 9

Plural Nouns

A plural noun is more than one
person, place, or thing

manners (MAN-urz) p. 7

vegetables
  (VEJ-tuh-buhlz) p. 11

Pronouns

A pronoun is a word that replaces a noun

he (HEE) p. 13

him (HIM) p. 19

I (EYE) pp. 9, 19

me (MEE) p. 15

she (SHEE)
  pp. 9, 15, 17, 21

something
  (SUHM-thing) pp. 5, 7

we (WEE) pp. 5, 7, 17

you (YOO) p. 13

22

Verbs

A verb is an action or being word

ask (ASK) pp. 5, 7, 21

asks (ASKSS)
pp. 13, 17, 19

be (BEE) p. 11

buy (BYE) p. 17

calls (KAWLZ) p. 15

chop (CHOP) p. 11

cooks (KUKSS) p. 9

follows (FOL-ohz) p. 15

have (HAV) p. 7

helping (HELP-ing) p. 11

is (IZ) pp. 11, 13

leave (LEEV) p. 21

like (LIKE) pp. 9, 21

make (MAKE) p. 17

making (MAKE-ing) p. 13

may (MAY) pp. 17, 19

pass (PASS) p. 13

say (SAY) p. 5

saying (SAY-ing) p. 7

says (SEZ) pp. 9, 11

should (SHUD) p. 21

shows (SHOHZ) p. 7

speak (SPEEK) p. 19

talks (TAWKSS) p. 19

wait (WATE) p. 15

wants (WONTSS) p. 17

watches (WOCH-iz) p. 9

would (WUD)
pp. 9, 13, 21

Adjectives

An adjective describes something

careful (KAIR-fuhl) p. 11

good (GUD) p. 7

her (HUR) pp. 9, 15

his (HIZ) pp. 11, 19

sharp (SHARP) p. 11

Adverbs

An adverb tells how, when, or where something happens

how (HOU) p. 21

out (OUT) p. 15

please (PLEEZ)
pp. 5, 7, 9, 11, 13, 15, 17, 19

23

Glossary

chop – to cut something with a knife.

jack-o-lantern – a pumpkin with a face carved into it and a candle inside, used at Halloween.

manners – polite behavior.

model – a small version of a larger object.